This
Imbolc Journal
Belongs To:

_____

Around February 2nd – Northern Hemisphere
Around August 2nd – Southern Hemisphere

Thanks for buying this journal!

I have lots more available on Amazon, including:

- Journals
- Undated Planners
- Composition Books (for school)
- Holiday themes
- Mermaids, Seahorses, starfish (I live near the beach, constant theme!)
- Florals & botanicals
- Hobby-themed journals for gardening, yoga, chakra-balancing, and other self-improvement topics – and some witchy stuff!

I'm Wanda, and Moon Magic Soul is my brand – welcome to my tribe!

Visit me:

www.moonmagicsoul.com

www.facebook.com/moonmagisoul

Using this Journal/Workbook

Welcome to the Season of Imbolc!

The pages are a way for you to explore and celebrate the season – to document your thoughts and feelings about Imbolc, and also to reflect on the past year, and keep moving through the new year!

Fill out what speaks to you – what you'd like to express. Ignore what doesn't fire you or interest you.

The first few pages are some month and week pages for personal planning. There are two months and six weeks – which gets you from Yuletide to just past Imbolc. If you already have a personal planner, you can art journal or ignore those pages.

Journaling – there are lots of journal prompts, have some fun with it! There are also some blank pages for you to doodle, scrapbook (paste or glue things) or make plans without lined pages.

Blessed be!

Sunday	Monday	Tuesday	Wednesday

MONTH

Thursday	Friday	Saturday

Sunday	Monday	Tuesday	Wednesday

MONTH

Thursday	Friday	Saturday

WEEK OF:

_____

Monday

Tuesday

Wednesday

Thursday

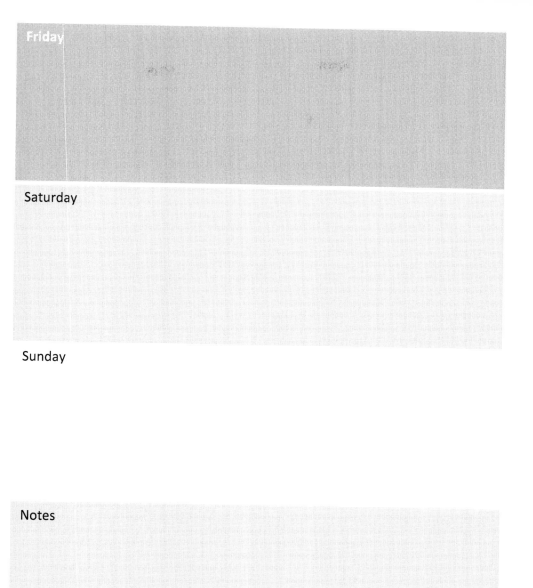

Friday

Saturday

Sunday

Notes

WEEK OF:

_____

Monday

Tuesday

Wednesday

Thursday

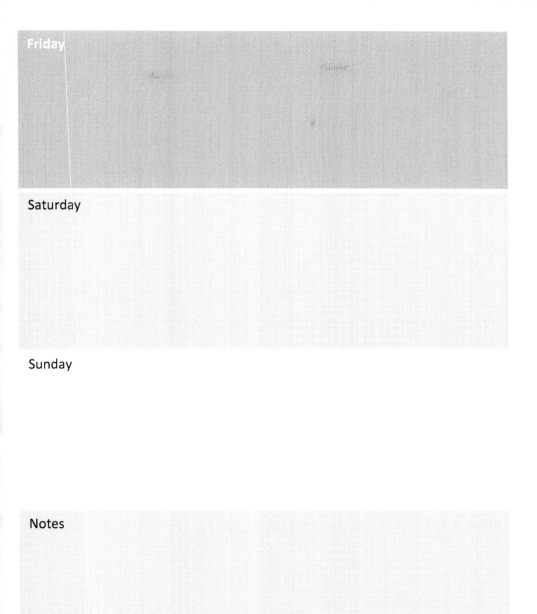

Friday

Saturday

Sunday

Notes

WEEK OF:

_____

Monday

Tuesday

Wednesday

Thursday

Friday

Saturday

Sunday

Notes

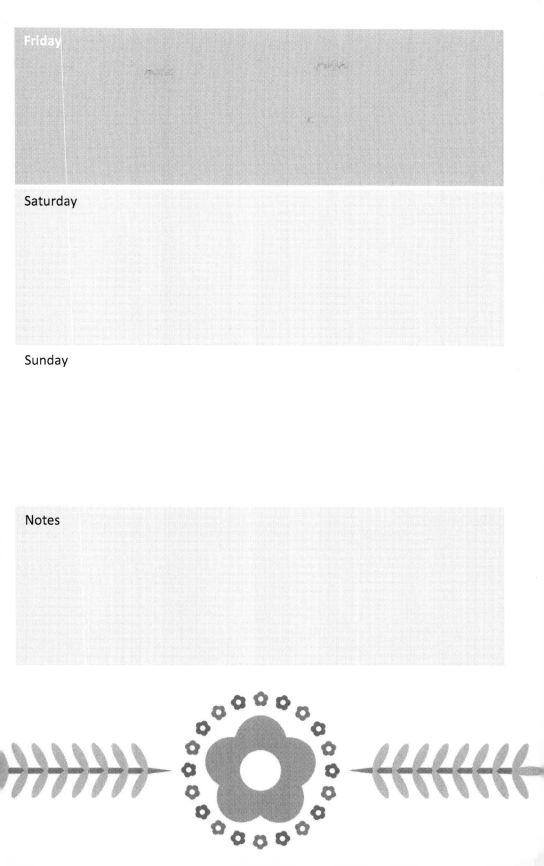

WEEK OF:

Monday

Tuesday

Wednesday

Thursday

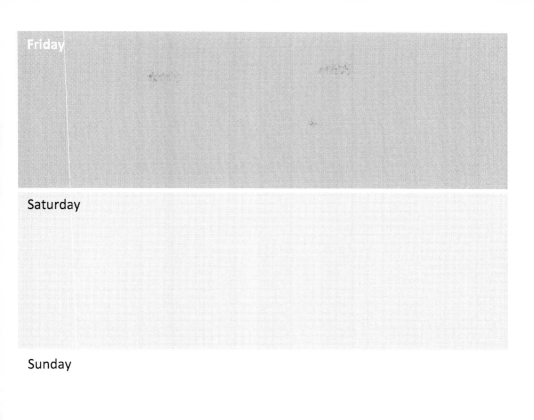

Friday

Saturday

Sunday

Notes

WEEK OF:

Monday

Tuesday

Wednesday

Thursday

Friday

Saturday

Sunday

Notes

WEEK OF:

_____

Monday

Tuesday

Wednesday

Thursday

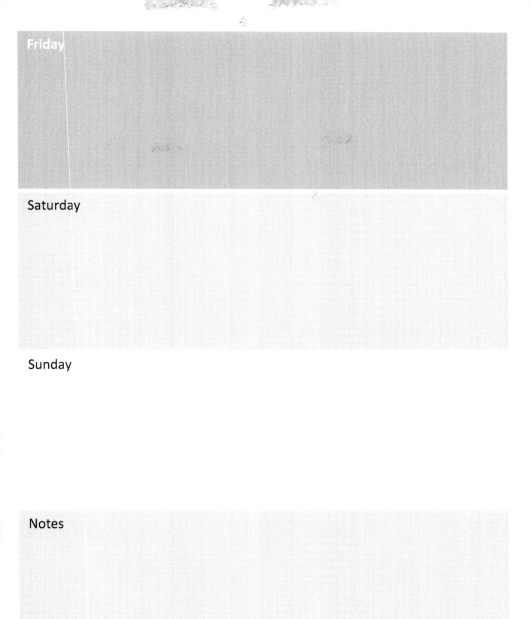

Friday

Saturday

Sunday

Notes

Meaning & Keywords

- ❑ Beginnings, awakening and renewal
- ❑ Cleansing/cleaning
- ❑ Sprouting seeds
- ❑ Fertility
- ❑ Transitions and changes

After celebrating Samhain and Yule, this is the season where the intentions set at year-end and Yuletide begin to grow – and maybe even blossom!

Some of us are still in "letting go" mode – use the weeks before Imbolc to finish that intention. Do some spring cleaning of your home, your mind, your body, and your witchy practices!

How have you celebrated during the cooler season of winter?

_____

_____

_____

_____

_____

_____

_____

_____

_____

_____

_____

_____

_____

_____

_____

_____

_____

_____

How has your life changed since last Imbolc?

_____

_____

_____

_____

_____

_____

_____

_____

_____

_____

_____

_____

_____

_____

_____

_____

_____

_____

What have you let go of?

How are your intentions growing and blossoming?

Have you planned or planted a spring garden yet?

Scents of the Season

- ❏ Cedar
- ❏ Peppermint
- ❏ Basil
- ❏ Freesia

Scenting Your Home

- ❏ Incense
- ❏ Candles
- ❏ Essential Oils with Scent Sticks
- ❏ Essential Oils in Diffusers
- ❏ Essential Oils rubbed on air vents
- ❏ Commercial plugs (no judgment)

What scents make you think of the coming spring?

How do you plan to use scent this season?

Decorations

- ❑ Colors – light green, pink, white, yellow and gold
- ❑ Dragons, robins and sheep
- ❑ Brigid's Cross (woven)
- ❑ Besom
- ❑ Wreaths

Do you decorate the entrance to your home to welcome the coming spring?

_____

_____

_____

Do you decorate the living space of your home for spring?

_____

_____

_____

What decorations are you seeing when you go out?

_____

_____

_____

_____

_____

_____

_____

_____

_____

_____

_____

_____

_____

_____

_____

_____

_____

_____

Foods

- ☐ Dried fruits & grains
- ☐ Potatoes
- ☐ Cornmeal
- ☐ Dried & salted meats
- ☐ Cheese
- ☐ Pickled or canned foods
- ☐ Nuts
- ☐ Eggs & Milk

Do you preserve food from the harvest season and eat it later in the year?

_____
_____
_____

What kind of dried and preserved foods do you like?

_____
_____
_____

Do you enjoy eating eggs and cheeses and drinking milk?

_____

_____

_____

_____

_____

_____

_____

_____

_____

_____

_____

_____

_____

_____

_____

_____

_____

_____

_____

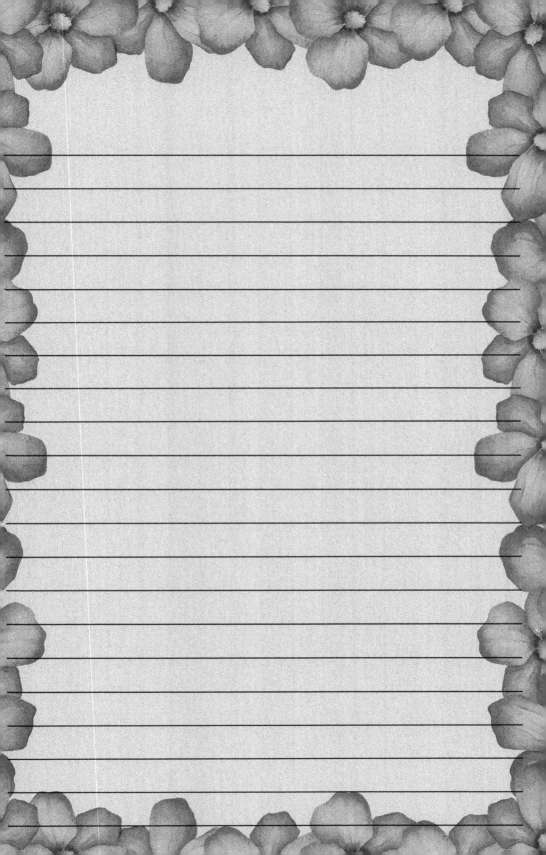

Activities for Imbolc

- ❑ Set up your altar – bring in elements of spring that is on the way!
- ❑ Decorate a besom with spring flowers and ribbons, hang in your home on or front door
- ❑ Take corn dollies made at Lammas and dress them as brides with scraps of lace and other remnants
- ❑ Weave a Brigid's Cross from straw
- ❑ Attend a blessing of the animals ceremony
- ❑ Spring clean your home
- ❑ Make candles

What items are you using to decorate your altar?

How often do you re-decorate your altar?

Sketch a new plan for your altar setup here:

Do you use a besom in your magickal practice?

Have you ever made corn dollies or Brigid's crosses as a craft?

Do you bless or do protection work for your animals and pets?

My familiar animals...

How are you beginning the spring cleaning process for your home?

How are you spring cleaning your mind and spirit?

_____

_____

_____

_____

_____

_____

_____

_____

_____

_____

_____

_____

_____

_____

_____

_____

_____

_____

_____

_____

Have you ever tried to make your own candles for your magickal work?

Ideas...

- ❑ Visit a local greenhouse and look for inspiration for your spring garden
- ❑ Plant late-blooming bulbs
- ❑ Sprout seeds in a sunny window-sill of your home to plant later in the spring
- ❑ Decorate tabletops and doorways with dried herbs and flowers
- ❑ Choose one room each week of the season, and clean all walls and surfaces. Move pictures and wall décor to different areas to refresh your home!

How are you planning to celebrate the Imbolc season?

_____

_____

_____

_____

_____

_____

_____

_____

_____

_____

_____

_____

_____

_____

_____

_____

_____

_____

_____

Natural Cleaning Ingredients

- ❑ white vinegar
- ❑ liquid castile soap
- ❑ natural salt
- ❑ baking soda
- ❑ borax
- ❑ washing soda
- ❑ hydrogen peroxide
- ❑ lemons
- ❑ microfiber cloths
- ❑ essential oils
- ❑ a spray bottle or two

Cleaning Recipes

Homemade All Purpose Cleaner
- 1 tsp borax
- 1/2 tsp washing soda
- 1 tsp liquid castile soap
- Essential oils of choice – I use 4 drops lemon, 4 drops lavender, and 10 drops orange
- 2 cups warm water
- Glass spray bottle for storage

Homemade Glass Cleaner
- 2 cups of water (distilled or filtered is best so it doesn't leave residue)
- 2 tablespoons vinegar
- 10 drops essential oil of choice- I use lemon (optional- but it helps cut the vinegar smell)

Homemade Wood Dusting Spray
- 1 cup water
- ½ cup vinegar (orange-infused for extra cleaning power and scent!)
- 2 TBSP oil (sunflower, grapeseed, fractionated coconut, or olive are my top choices)
- 10 drops lemon essential oil
- 5 drops cedarwood essential oil

SPRING CLEANING WEEK ONE

What room/area are you cleaning?:

_____

Are you moving any decorations around?:

_____

What week are you doing the cleaning?:

_____

- ❑ Ceiling swept & light fixtures cleaned
- ❑ Walls wiped down
- ❑ Doorframes wiped down
- ❑ Baseboards washed
- ❑ Floors cleaned
- ❑ Cabinets & furniture wiped down
- ❑ Window treatments cleaned
- ❑ _____
- ❑ _____
- ❑ _____

_____

_____

_____

_____

_____

_____

_____

SPRING CLEANING WEEK TWO

What room/area are you cleaning?:

_____

Are you moving any decorations around?:

_____

What week are you doing the cleaning?:

_____

- ❑ Ceiling swept & light fixtures cleaned
- ❑ Walls wiped down
- ❑ Doorframes wiped down
- ❑ Baseboards washed
- ❑ Floors cleaned
- ❑ Cabinets & furniture wiped down
- ❑ Window treatments cleaned
- ❑ _____
- ❑ _____
- ❑ _____

_____

_____

_____

_____

_____

_____

SPRING CLEANING WEEK THREE

What room/area are you cleaning?:

_____

Are you moving any decorations around?:

_____

What week are you doing the cleaning?:

_____

- ❑ Ceiling swept & light fixtures cleaned
- ❑ Walls wiped down
- ❑ Doorframes wiped down
- ❑ Baseboards washed
- ❑ Floors cleaned
- ❑ Cabinets & furniture wiped down
- ❑ Window treatments cleaned
- ❑ _____
- ❑ _____
- ❑ _____

_____

_____

_____

_____

_____

_____

_____

SPRING CLEANING WEEK FOUR

What room/area are you cleaning?:

_____

Are you moving any decorations around?:

_____

What week are you doing the cleaning?:

_____

- ❑ Ceiling swept & light fixtures cleaned
- ❑ Walls wiped down
- ❑ Doorframes wiped down
- ❑ Baseboards washed
- ❑ Floors cleaned
- ❑ Cabinets & furniture wiped down
- ❑ Window treatments cleaned
- ❑ _____
- ❑ _____
- ❑ _____

_____

_____

_____

_____

_____

_____

_____

SPRING CLEANING WEEK FIVE

What room/area are you cleaning?:

_____

Are you moving any decorations around?:

_____

What week are you doing the cleaning?:

_____

- ❑ Ceiling swept & light fixtures cleaned
- ❑ Walls wiped down
- ❑ Doorframes wiped down
- ❑ Baseboards washed
- ❑ Floors cleaned
- ❑ Cabinets & furniture wiped down
- ❑ Window treatments cleaned
- ❑ _____
- ❑ _____
- ❑ _____

_____

_____

_____

_____

_____

_____

SPRING CLEANING WEEK SIX

What room/area are you cleaning?:

_____

Are you moving any decorations around?:

_____

What week are you doing the cleaning?:

_____

- ❑ Ceiling swept & light fixtures cleaned
- ❑ Walls wiped down
- ❑ Doorframes wiped down
- ❑ Baseboards washed
- ❑ Floors cleaned
- ❑ Cabinets & furniture wiped down
- ❑ Window treatments cleaned
- ❑ _____
- ❑ _____
- ❑ _____

_____

_____

_____

_____

_____

_____

_____

_____

Spellwork & Rituals:

- ❑ Dedicate any new magickal tools that you've acquired or made over the winter
- ❑ Cleanse your home by burning sage or spritzing a homemade sage and other essential oil spray
- ❑ Ward your windows and doorways with protection work
- ❑ Do spellwork and rituals to enhance your health and beauty – bathe with herbs and oils, use lotion and cream to write sigils on your face and body!
- ❑ Continue the releasing and manifesting work that begin at Samhain and Yuletide
- ❑ Use tarot cards, runes, scrying or other divinatory tools to seek guidance about ongoing year; write a summary of your process and any messages received

What bad habits have you banished already this year?

How have you honoured the Mother Goddess with new growth this year?

Do you have a social group that you can celebrate the sabbats and esbats with? Why or why not?

What are your favorite divination tools? Why?

Divination –
Looking Forward:

The next pages are spaces for you to record by month what your favorite divination tools are telling you about your upcoming year.

Make it a habit to review your reading on a monthly basis, and make comments about what has unfolded. Leave space in between for future journaling and exploration!

Month 1
The Season of Imbolc

Month 1
Reflections

Month 2
The Season of Spring

Month 2
Reflections

_____

_____

_____

_____

_____

_____

_____

_____

_____

_____

_____

_____

_____

_____

_____

_____

_____

Month 3
The Season of Ostara

Month 3
Reflections

Month 4
The Season of Beltane

Month 4
Reflections

Month 5
The Season of Litha

Month 5
Reflections

Month 6
The Season of Summer

Month 6
Reflections

_____

_____

_____

_____

_____

_____

_____

_____

_____

_____

_____

_____

_____

_____

_____

_____

_____

_____

Month 7
The Season of Lammas

Month 7
Reflections

Month 8
The Season of Late Summer

Month 8
Reflections

Month 9
The Season of Samhain

Month 9
Reflections

Month 10
The Year Begins

Month 10
Reflections

Month 11
The Season of Yule

Month 11
Reflections

Month 12
The Season of Winter

Month 12
Reflections

_____

_____

_____

_____

_____

_____

_____

_____

_____

_____

_____

_____

_____

_____

_____

_____

_____

_____

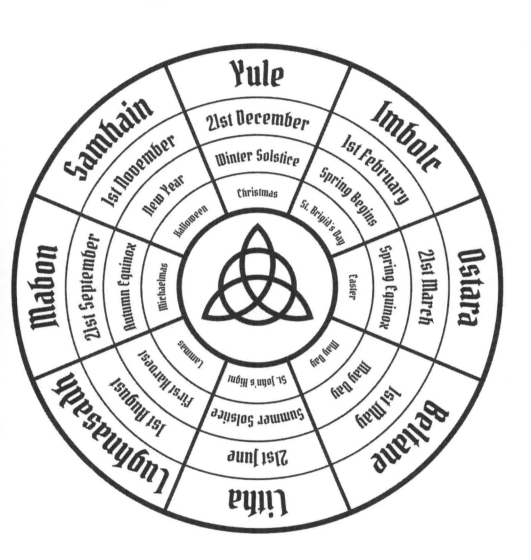

Thanks for buying this journal!
I have lots more available on Amazon, including:

- Journals
- Undated Planners
- Composition Books (for school)
- Holiday themes
- Mermaids, Seahorses, starfish (I live near the beach, constant theme!)
- Florals & botanicals
- Hobby-themed journals for gardening, yoga, chakra-balancing, and other self-improvement topics – and some witchy stuff!

I'm Wanda, and Moon Magic Soul is my brand – welcome to my tribe!

Visit me:

www.moonmagicsoul.com

www.facebook.com/moonmagisoul

Printed in Great Britain
by Amazon